# OnBoard
ACADEMICS

# Nouns

© 2015 OnBoard Academics, Inc
Portsmouth, NH
800-596-3175
www.onboardacademics.com
ISBN: 978-1-63096-030-8

---

OnBoard Academic's books are specifically designed to be used as printed workbooks or as on-screen instruction. Each page offers focused exercises and students quickly master topics with enough proficiency to move on to the next level.

OnBoard Academic's lessons are used in over 25,000 classrooms to rave reviews. Our lessons are aligned to the most recent governmental standards and are updated from time to time as standards change. Correlation documents are located on our website. Our lessons are created, edited and evaluated by educators to ensure top quality and real life success.

Interactive lessons for digital whiteboards, mobile devices, and PCs are available at www.onboardacademics.com. These interactive lessons make great additions to our books.

---

You can always reach us at customerservice@onboardacademics.com.

# Nouns

**Key Vocabulary**

person

place

thing

**Nouns**
A noun is a person, place or thing.

**Sort the nouns.**

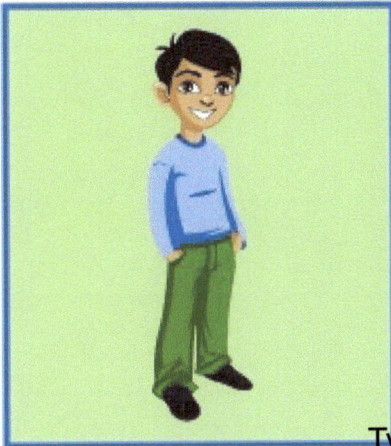

Type to enter text

| person | place | thing |
|--------|-------|-------|

| person | place | thing |
|--------|-------|-------|
|        |       |       |
|        |       |       |
|        |       |       |

| pilot | teacher | principal |
| house | computer | apartment |
| ruler | book | ballpark |

**Can you think of some nouns for these three categories?**

| person | place | thing |
|--------|-------|-------|
|        |       |       |
|        |       |       |
|        |       |       |

_____

**Circle the nouns.**

Twinkle, twinkle, little star,

How I wonder what you are.

Up above the world so high,

Like a diamond in the sky.

Twinkle, twinkle, little star,

How I wonder what you are.

**Use the context of the paragraph to fill in the missing nouns.**
Suggestions are listed in blue boxes.

My _____ and I go to the same _____ ,

so we ride the _____ together.

The _____ thinks that we look alike and

sometimes gets our _____ mixed up.

Thankfully, this doesn't happen at _____ !

| school | names | bus | home | hand |
|--------|-------|-----|------|------|
| driver | room | dog | sister | cookie |

Name_____

## Nouns Quiz

1. A noun is a person, place or thing.  True or false?

2. Circle the group of words containing only nouns.
   a. magazine, long, read
   b. big, computer, type
   c. swim, noisy, pool
   d. sand, beach, ocean

3. Most sentences have nouns.  True or false?

4. Fill in the blank.  My _____ has fleas.
   a. happy
   b. warm
   c. dog
   d. erasure

5. Fill in the blank. We saw a zebra in the _____.
   a. zoo
   b. supermarket
   c. farm
   d. treehouse

# Plural Nouns

**Key Vocabulary**

plural nouns

**Match the nouns to the picture.**

## A noun is a person, place or thing.

| window | flowers | cat | kids |
|--------|---------|-----|------|
| table | buildings | goldfish | trees |

**Plural Nouns**

> Many plural nouns have an **-s** at the **end**.

 The teacher helped the student.

 The teacher**s** helped the student.

_____

**Make the noun plural.**

 paper_____

 pencil_____

 book_____

 crayon_____

**Plural nouns that end in -es**

> Add an **-es** to plural nouns that end in **-sh**, **-ch**, **-s**, or **-x**.

| box | watch | dish | kiss |
|-----|-------|------|------|
| boxes | watches | dishes | kisses |

_____

**Will the plural end in an -s or an -es?**

glass ☐

snake ☐

box ☐

basket ☐

dish ☐

**s**

**es**

**Irregular Plural Nouns**

| Some plural nouns **do not** end in -s. |
| --- |

| singular | plural |
| --- | --- |
| one child | four **children** |
| one tooth | ten **teeth** |
| one mouse | five **mice** |
| one sheep | eight **sheep** |

---

**Sort the nouns by their plural form.**

| -s ending | -es ending | irregular |
| --- | --- | --- |
|  |  |  |
|  |  |  |

| buzz | ox | picture |
| --- | --- | --- |
| woman | loss | toaster |

**Plural Nouns Crossword**

Complete the crossword with the plural form of the noun.

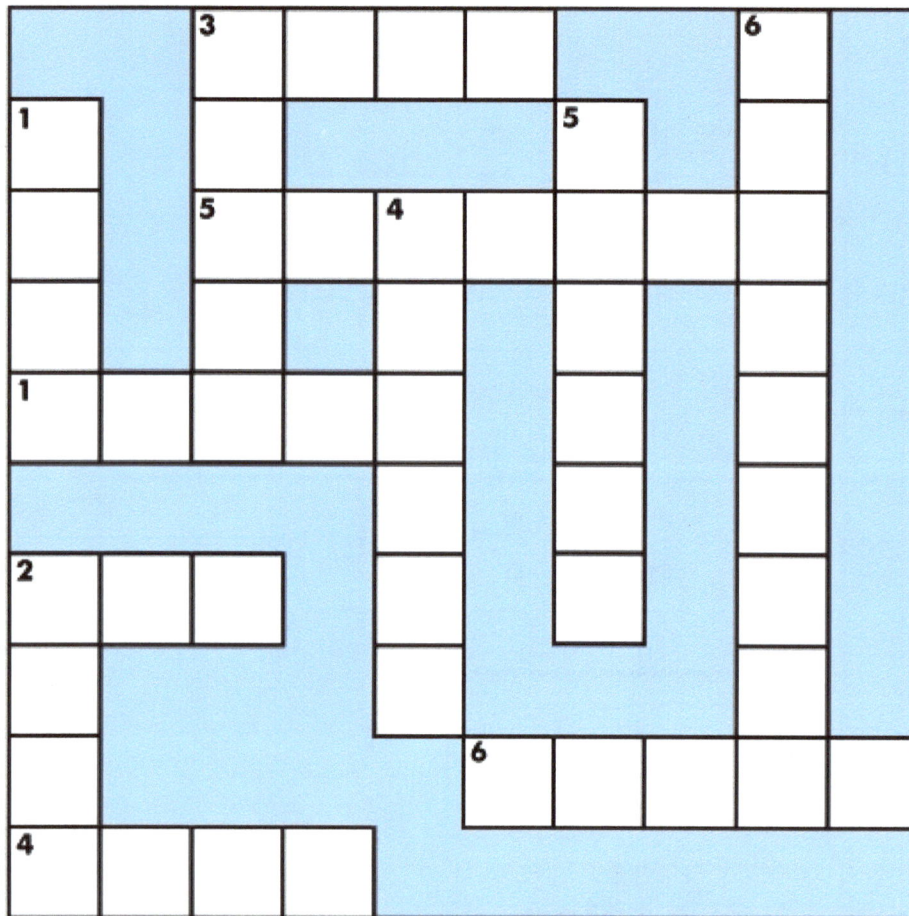

**ACROSS**

1. rose
2. man
3. bat
4. eel
5. sister
6. goose

**DOWN**

1. deer
2. mouse
3. bus
4. sash
5. person
6. baseball

Name_____

## Plural Nouns Quiz

1. Most plural nouns end with -s. True or false?

2. What is the plural form of cat?
   a. cates
   b. cats
   c. cat
   d. caten

3. What is the plural form of witch?
   a. witch
   b. witches
   c. witchs
   d. witchypoo

4. Which is the incorrect plural noun?
   a. fish
   b. pumpkins
   c. bookes
   d. dresses

5. What is the plural form of catch?
   a. catch
   b. catchs
   c. catches
   d. catchings

# Possessive Nouns

## Key Vocabulary

noun

possessive noun

apostrophe

singular

plural

> A **noun** is a person, place or thing. A **possessive noun** shows ownership and is formed by adding a properly placed apostrophe.

**Complete the phrase.**

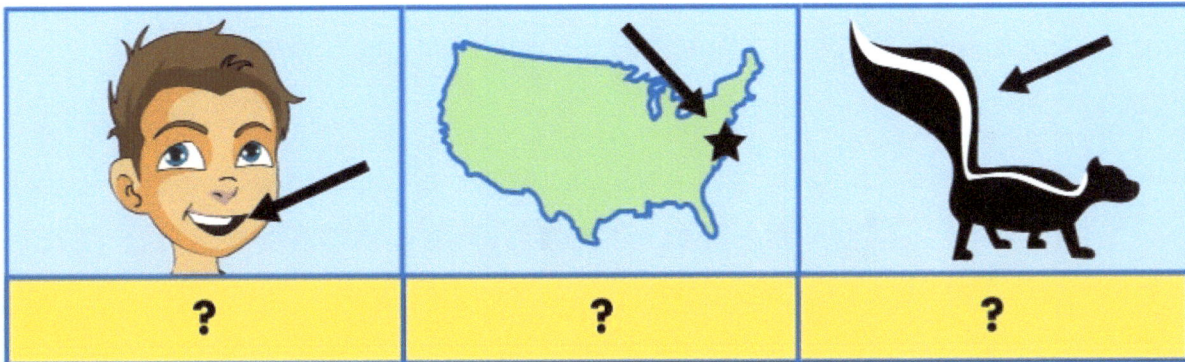

| ? | ? | ? |

Owen's _____    America's _____    Skunk's _____

| capital | mouth | tail |

**Possessive Singular Nouns**

A **possessive singular noun** shows that something belongs to *one person or thing* and is formed by adding an *apostrophe and -s* to the noun.

Complete the last sentence to show that the eggs belong to the bird.

The pencil that belongs to the girl.

The girl's pencil

The eggs that belong to the bird.

The bird  eggs.

**Complete the possessive singular noun form.**

| | | |
|---|---|---|
| desk of the teacher | = _____ | desk |
| the color of the sky | = _____ | color |
| breath of a dragon | = _____ | breath |
| the name of the dog | = _____ | name |
| title of the book | = _____ | title |

_____

**Complete the sentences with the possessive form of the noun.**

Mia          _____ school had a talent show.

David          _____ parents came to watch him play the guitar.

music          They applauded the _____ beautiful melody.

**Possessive Plural Nouns**

# A possessive plural noun shows that something belongs to *more than one person or thing* and is formed by adding an *apostrophe*.

Complete the possessive plural noun in the last sentence.

**The bike that belongs to the boys.**

**The boys' bike**

**The tires that belong to the trucks.**

**The            tires**

**Fill in the blank with the correct possessive plural pronoun.**

The [_____] branches shook in the wind.

The [_____] pages were yellowed.

The [_____] fish lived in a big aquarium.

| books' | sisters' | trees's |
| book's | sisters's | trees' |

**Possessive plural and possessive singular nouns.**

Create either possessive singular or possessive plural nouns by adding an apostrophe (') or an apostrophe s ('s) to each box.

| Alison | | bike |
|--------|--|------|
| singers | | voices |
| eagle | | nest |
| children | | toes |
| musician | | talent |
| libraries | | books |
| men | | shoes |

www.onboardacademics.com

**Sort these sentences.**

| correct possessive noun | incorrect possessive noun |
|---|---|
|  |  |
|  |  |
|  |  |

The flowers's petals are red.        The couch's fabric was worn.

The dogs' bark was playful.        Mias' hair is very long.

The seagulls' cries were loud.        The dolphin's pool was big.

Name_____

## Possessive Nouns Quiz

1. True or false?  The possessive form of a singular noun ends with 's?

2. Fill in the blank.  The _____ opened their gifts at the party.  boys'  boy's  boys

3. Fill in the blank.  I went to my _____ house after school.  friends  friend's  friends'

4. Did you see _____ new haircut?  Davids  David's  Davids'

5. The two _____ baseball cards were in an album.  brothers  brothers'  brother's

6. Put a check next to the sentence not written correctly.
   a. The whale's pool was very large.
   b. My friend's shirt is green.
   c. 9 and 11 are my son's ages.
   d. My parents' room is full of books.

          www.onboardacademics.com

# Nouns, Plural Nouns and Pronouns

## Key Vocabulary

noun

pronoun

singular

plural

**Nouns**

# A noun is a person, place or thing and is often the subject of a sentence.

---

Draw a line to connect the noun in the sentence with the correct description.

thing

**Anthony** is ten years old.

person

The **library** is open today.

place

A **hammer** is a useful tool.

**Fill in the missing nouns.**

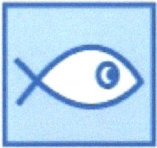

The class is taking a trip to the [ ].

[ ] ate his [ ] on the [ ].

The [ ] was having a huge sale.

Everyone filed down the [ ] when the [ ] sounded at the elementary [ ].

| ice cream | school | stairs | alarm |
| swing set | James | aquarium | store |

**Plural nouns that end in -s or -es are shown below.**

candle

candles

dish

dishes

couch

couches

glass

glasses

ax

axes

quiz

quizzes

**Write the plural form of each noun.**

penguin

dress

cousin

taxes

bush

bill

**Nouns that end in  -y.**

> ### For nouns that end in -y:
> ### "Change the y to i and add es!"

| baby | cherry | candy |
|---|---|---|
| | | |
| bab**ies** | cherr**ies** | cand**ies** |

**Make these nouns plural by adding one of three endings.**

1. c a k e
2. p e n n y
3. d o o r
4. c h u r c h
5. c i t y
6. b o x
7. l a d y

s

e s

i e s

**Irregular Plural Nouns**

| singular | |
|---|---|
| | child |
| | tooth |
| | sheep |
| | woman |

Can you select the correct pluralization for these irregular plural nouns? Circle your answer.

| plural | |
|---|---|
| | child, childs, children, childes |
| | tooth, toothes, teeth, toothies |
| | sheep, herd |
| | woman, ladies girls, women |

**Plural Nouns**

Circle the irregular plural noun in each sentence and then write the singular form in the box.

James caught four fish yesterday.

There are 5,280 feet in a mile.

Those moose aren't afraid of the hikers.

Arizona has a lot of cacti.

Mia saw two deer in her backyard.

The pet store is selling albino mice.

**Incorrect Plurals**

Underline the incorrect plurals.

## My Favorite Thinges
### by Tori Kennedy

Sunny skys and sandy beaches

Homemade fries and Georgia peachies.

Friends and familys, cats and dogs

Me and James catching froges.

Bedtime storys then counting sheep,

Goodnight kissies, it's time to sleep.

**Pronouns**

Anthony is in the fourth grade.
**He** is the student body president.

A **pronoun** can replace a noun in a sentence and needs to agree in number and gender.

Mia is meeting Tori at the mall.
**They** are going to go shopping.

The box is really big.
**It** can hold a lot of stuff.

**Complete the sentence with the missing pronoun.**

| | pronouns |
|---|---|
| The people clapped ☐ hands in applause. | I |
| Owen, when does ☐ vacation start? | we |
| Mom and ☐ picked up some groceries. | my |
| It was Mia's job to clean the sink, not ☐. | mine |
| Tori and I have to finish ☐ homework. | us |
| Is ☐ waiting for her bus to come in? | she |
| | his |
| | you |
| | your |
| | our |
| | it |
| | they |
| | their |

## Nouns, Plural Nouns and Pronouns Quiz

1. Nouns and pronouns can be people, places or things. True or false?

2. Circle the noun in this sentence: "I can't wait to see the zebras at the zoo."

3. What is the singular form of the plural noun mice?
   a. moose
   b. mices
   c. mouse
   d. mise

4. Complete the sentence with the correct pronoun:
   _____ have matching shirts.
   a. He
   b. She
   c. They
   d. It

5. Complete the sentence with the correct noun: We ate juicy _____ for our snack.
   a. peach
   b. peachs
   c. peaches
   d. peachies

www.ingramcontent.com/pod-product-compliance
Lightning Source LLC
Chambersburg PA
CBHW060816090426
42737CB00002B/77